A New True Book

THE ONONDAGA

By Jill D. Duvall

CHILDRENS PRESS ®
CHICAGO

PHOTO CREDITS

The Bettmann Archive—9 (right), 28, 31

© Reinhard Brucker—24; © Milwaukee Public Museum, 16 (left), 20; © Field Museum, 16 (right)

© John Dowling—4, 40 (right)

© Mike Greenlar—27 (2 photos), 41 (left)

Historical Pictures Service—8

North Wind Picture Archives—9 (left), 10, 14

© Mike Okoniewski—44 (bottom)

Photo courtesy of Smithsonian Institution of the National Museum of the American Indian—13 (right)

SuperStock International, Inc.—19

UPI/Bettmann—7, 37

© 1990 Steve Wall—Cover, 2, 13, 17, 23, 33, 34 (2 photos), 39, 40 (left), 41 (right), 43 (2 photos), 44 (top), 45

Cover—Onondaga children, mothers, and grandmother

A young Onondaga at the Green Corn Festival

© 1990 Steve Wall

Library of Congress Cataloging-in-Publication Data

Duvall, Jill D.
    The Onondaga / by Jill D. Duvall.
        p.   cm. — (A New true book)
    Includes index.
    Summary: Describes the history, culture, and current fortunes of Onondaga Indians.
    ISBN 0-516-01126-X
    1. Onondaga Indians—Juvenile literature.
[1. Onondaga Indians.   2. Indians of North America.]   I.   Title.
E99.O58D88   1991   91-8894
973'.04975—dc20   CIP
                                           AC

TABLE OF CONTENTS

The modern city of Syracuse, New York, lies on the shores of Onondaga Lake.

PEOPLE ON THE HILLS

The Oswego River winds
for many miles between
Lake Ontario and
Onondaga Lake. From
below the river, say the
Onondaga, they first came
onto Turtle Island—North
America.

The Onondaga called
themselves People on the
Hills. Their villages were
built on hillsides. Often

two villages were built
near each other for
protection. The houses and
the fences around them
were made of wood.

The earliest descriptions
we have of an Onondaga
village were written in
1654 by French Jesuit
missionaries. The

The Native Americans called the French Jesuits "Black Robes."

Onondaga "prepared a mat" for the visitors. This meant they were invited to stay if they wished. Hospitality was very important to the Onondaga.

A longhouse had a frame of wooden poles sunk in the ground and curved at the top to form a roof. The frame was covered with sheets of tree bark.

What the Europeans saw amazed them. Many long buildings covered with bark stood in clusters. Around the village were large fields. Rows and rows of vegetables had been planted. From the surrounding meadows and forests, the Onondaga had collected fruits, nuts, and berries. The Jesuits had never seen many of these foods before. Clean water, animals, and fish were nearby. Life was good.

Native Americans spearing fish from a canoe (below) and sowing seeds for food crops (right)

A chief
speaks at
an Iroquois
Council.

THE PEACEMAKER

Native Americans had lived in this part of North America for many centuries. There had been many wars. Blood feuds existed with almost every group.

One day, a young Onondaga chief named Aionwatha arrived at a Mohawk village. He wore white beads on strings around his neck. This meant he came in peace.

The Mohawk leaders greeted him. When Aionwatha told them of the deaths of all his family, they felt very sad for him.

Another visitor had just come to that same village.

The Mohawks and the visitor held a ceremony to help the young chief feel better. They called it the Condolence Ceremony. It is still performed to pay respects to chiefs who have died. Today during the ceremony, new chiefs are "raised up."

After the first Condolence Ceremony, the visitor told Aionwatha his plan for peace. Aionwatha wanted very much to have peace among his people.

The Condolence Cane (left) is still used at the Condolence Ceremony. An Onondaga chief (right), holding a wampum belt, photographed in 1907.

Together they went to the home of the head Onondaga chief. His name was Tadodaho. When they told him of the plan, he became very angry. It

13

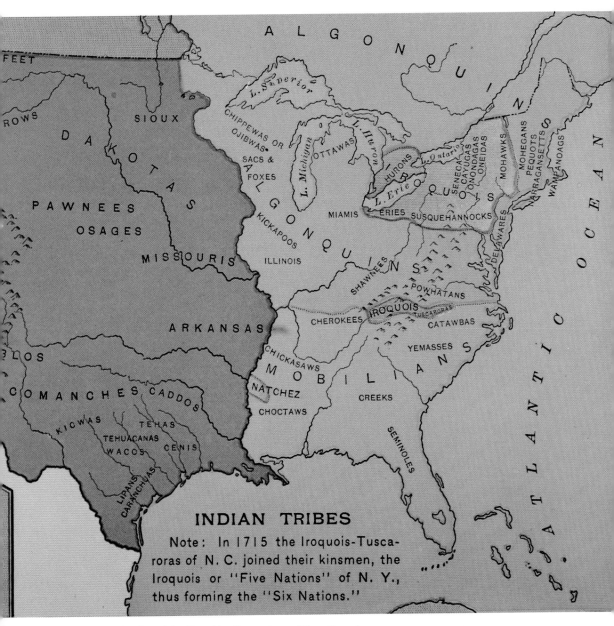

INDIAN TRIBES

Note: In 1715 the Iroquois-Tusca-roras of N. C. joined their kinsmen, the Iroquois or "Five Nations" of N. Y., thus forming the "Six Nations."

The Iroquois lived in the Northeastern Woodlands of what is now the United States.

took them a long time to win him over.

After years of hard work, five Indian nations agreed to stop warring against each other. They were the Seneca, Mohawk, Cayuga, Oneida, and Onondaga. From that time, the man who brought the plan was called the Peacemaker. The Five Nations called themselves *Haudenosaunee*, (ho•dee•no•SAW•nee), the People of the Longhouse.

The Onondaga were

The Onondaga ate with wooden spoons (left). They chopped weeds from their gardens with hoes that had blades made of elk's antlers (right).

made Keepers of the Fire for the Five Nations. Wherever the Onondaga were, that was where the Council Fire of the Five Nations would be kindled. Tadodaho was chosen to call together the Grand Councils. He was called "first among equals."

Today, Six Nations Grand Council meetings are held at Onondaga National Territory in New York State.

SHARING POWER

The Peacemaker had many good ideas. Each nation would rule itself. Women and men shared power. Everyone had to agree on decisions in the Grand Councils. Only then

17

did they become laws. In councils, each nation had several representatives but only one vote.

Peace chiefs, or *sachems*, were chosen by the women who were heads of families. These women were called Clan Mothers. Fourteen of the first 50 chiefs selected were Onondaga.

Chiefs were replaced only when they died or if they did not follow the wishes of their people.

Sachems of the Haudenosaunee Council meeting with the Europeans

Special persons called orators spoke at council meetings. Records say that the speeches ended with *Hiro-koue*, "I have said it." To the French, that sounded like "Iroquois."

That is how the Haudenosaunee became known to non-Indians as the Five Nations Confederacy of the Iroquois.

The Peacemaker and the

The Iroquois made strings of colored beads called wampum. The beads were often woven into belts in patterns that told a story.

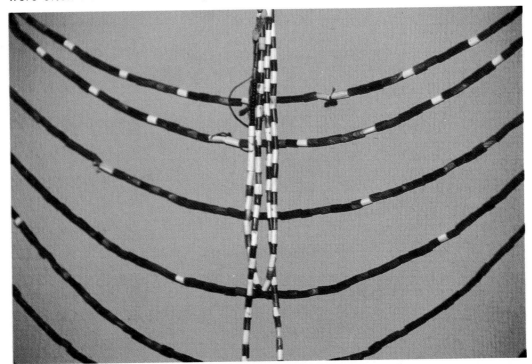

first chiefs planted a pine tree on the shores of Onondaga Lake. This tree is the symbol of the Confederacy.

People who accepted the Great Law of Peace would find shelter under the Tree of Peace. In the early 1700s, the Tuscarora nation was adopted by the Haudenosaunee. Now the Confederacy had six nations.

VILLAGE LIFE

Women owned the longhouses in an Onondaga village. Each longhouse was home to a number of families.

There was a door at each end of the longhouse. Totems, or pictures, of the clan whose members lived inside were hung over each longhouse door.

Under the clan system, members of the same clan

Onondaga women gather in the home of Faith Keeper and Clan Mother Audrey Shenandoah to practice traditional songs.

were related through the female members. The women who lived in a longhouse were sisters, mothers, or daughters of the same family.

23

The families slept on furs spread on low wooden platforms at the sides of the longhouse.

In the longhouse, every family had its own cooking fire. The fires were placed down the center of the longhouse.

Several clans lived in a village. When a marriage

was arranged, husband
and wife could not be
from the same clan.
Fathers and their children
belonged to different clans.
Children were members of
their mother's clan.

The Onondaga clans are
the Wolf, Turtle, Snipe,
Beaver, Hawk, Deer, Eel,
and Bear.

The Onondaga played lacrosse. Long ago, it was a very rough sport. There were almost no rules. Goalposts were sometimes miles apart. The French thought the stick used to play the game looked like a bishop's crosier. They called the game *la crosse*.

In the game, each side was made up of many players. Once the game started, it could be played for days.

The nations have

Alf Jacques (left), an Onondaga, carves
lacrosse sticks from hickory wood. A net will
fill the curved end of the stick.
Iroquois children (above) in action
during a lacrosse game.

separate lacrosse teams
today. There is also a
team called the "Iroquois
Nationals" that competes
in international games. The
game is very different now,
but it is still very exciting.

27

At first, the French fur trappers and the Native Americans were friends.

A LAND DIVIDED

For a long time, many of the Europeans and the Northeast Woodland nations were friends. They trapped and traded together. Some Europeans married Indian women and raised families. The Iroquois adopted a number of non-Indians into their nations.

Unfortunately, the friendship between the French and the Onondaga did not last long. Soldiers, under orders from Governor Frontenac of Canada, destroyed the Onondaga villages. The last village was destroyed in 1696.

PROBLEMS WITH NEWCOMERS

Dutch, English, and French fur trappers had needed the Indians to help them. Most of the early troubles started over the fur trade. Later, the Europeans fought each other for land.

The Native Americans did not understand the behavior of the new Americans. Land had always been owned by the whole nation. Hunting

European fur companies competed to trade with the Native Americans.

grounds were open to members of the Confederacy and to other friends. But the Americans thought land could be owned. They passed laws to protect their land.

Very soon, there was not enough land for everybody.

Finally, the Six Nations
disagreed over the American
Revolution. The Onondaga and
three other Iroquois tribes
fought on the British side
against the Americans.

After the war, many treaties
were made. Native
Americans were soon
outnumbered, and most of
their land had been stolen
or given to settlers, states,

Tadodaho—Chief Leon Shenandoah—joins other Six Nations chiefs to remember the Canandaigua Treaty of 1794, which guaranteed lands to the nations of the Iroquois.

or land companies. The Native Americans were badly cheated in many of the deals.

33

Onondaga National Territory today.
At the right, Onondaga Creek, which
is part of the territory, runs
through the city of Syracuse.

THE ONONDAGA TODAY

The Northeastern
Woodland nations now
have only a few small
areas for their territories.

34

Onondaga National Territory is located south of Syracuse, New York. It covers 7,300 acres of the Onondaga's original land. About 2,000 people live there.

The Six Nations councils are held at the home of the Onondaga. The names of the first Confederacy chiefs are handed down, as they used to be, to each chief who replaces the one before him.

There is still a chief named Tadodaho. Stories

of the first Tadodaho say
he was very mean.
Everyone was afraid of
him. Today, the chief
named Tadodaho is a
gentle man with a quiet
voice. He is also known as
Chief Leon Shenandoah.
People of the Six Nations
respect him. They know he
works hard and "keeps the
council fire burning."

The problems are still
land and water rights. Today's
Tadodaho can be just as
fierce as the first one was.

New York education commissioner Thomas Sobol (left) meets with Chief Leon Shenandoah (center) and Chief Irving Powless, Jr. (right), as twelve wampum belts are returned to the Onondaga nation. The belts are records of Onondaga history.

His weapons, though, are words. As always, warriors take over when the peace chiefs cannot solve problems. Now, treaties and courts are the weapons of the Onondaga.

THE SACRED EARTH

The Iroquois people have
many different religions.
They also respect other
people's beliefs. Many of the
Onondaga are members
of the Longhouse Religion.
It is called *Gaiwiio*, which
means "the Good Word."

Onondaga keep the
traditional way of life by
celebrating the yearly
cycle of the seasons. The
celebrations begin and end
with prayers of thanksgiving
to the Creator of Life.

Onondaga performing the ancient songs and dances at the Green Corn Festival at Onondaga National Territory

Some of the ceremonies are Green Corn, Strawberry, Planting, Harvest, and Midwinter. The last is the most important. Thanks are given for all things of nature. Ancient dances and songs are performed.

Chief Oren Lyons (far right) made this painting of Iroquois dancers (right)

Ceremonies must be carefully prepared. Special people, called Keepers of the Faith, are selected for this. Chief Oren Lyons is a Faith Keeper and a university professor. He spends a great deal of time helping his

Above: Chiefs Leon Shenandoah, Irving Powless, Jr., and Oren Lyons (left to right), holding a wampum belt. Right: Chief Oren Lyons displays his Haudenosaunee passport.

nation and other native peoples around the world. The Iroquois now have many diplomats. They issue their own passports, which include the clan names of the owners. Many nations around the world honor the passports.

41

TWENTIETH-CENTURY LIFE

Onondaga families now usually live in single-family houses. There are elementary schools in the National Territory. High-school students attend local public schools.

There is a new Council House made of logs. Stoves have replaced the open fires of long ago. The affairs of the Onondaga are managed by chiefs who are chosen in the old way.

Left: Houses at Onondaga Territory.
Right: A class at an elementary school
in the territory is taught by
an Onondaga teacher.

Very few Onondaga are farmers today. They work in industry and business like their non-Indian neighbors.

Gravel pits are located within the borders of Onondaga. The gravel is sold to local builders.

Old people of the Six Nations are respected and cared for by their Onondaga neighbors.

United States and New York State funds due to the Onondaga by treaty rights are still paid. The payments are made mostly for Onondaga lands taken by others.

Self-help groups have been organized. There are helpers when houses must be built or repaired. Planting and harvesting work is often done in groups. People who are sick know they are not

Chief Vince Johnson and his children carry "Treaty Salt." This salt is given to the Onondaga each year under the terms of a treaty. The salt is payment for the land that the city of Syracuse, New York, stands on.

forgotten. Older residents find cut firewood outside their homes during the bitter winters.

The Onondaga spirit proves that having a lot of land is not what makes a nation great.

WORDS YOU SHOULD KNOW

adopted (uh • DAHPT • tid) — taken in; made a part of a group

ancient (AIN • shint) — very old

ceremony (SAIR • ih • moh • nee) — a celebration or a religious service held to show respect or thankfulness

clan (KLAN) — a group of families that have the same ancestors

condolence (kun • DOHL • ince) — expressing sorrow and sympathy for a person's loss

confederacy (kun • FED • er • uh • see) — a union of nations, states, or people joined together for some purpose

council (KOWN • sil) — a meeting held to discuss problems and to decide a course of action

crosier (KROH • zjee • er) — a long wooden staff that is bent over into a loop at the top

cycle (SY • kil) — a complete set of events that keep repeating in the same order

diplomat (DIP • loh • mat) — a person who represents his or her government in another country

feud (FYOOD) — fighting; a quarrel, especially one between two groups of people

hospitality (hahss • pih • TAL • ih • tee) — a generous and friendly way of treating strangers

industry (IN • duss • tree) — the manufacture of goods such as automobiles and machinery

international (in • ter • NASH • uh • nil) — between countries

missionaries (MISH • un • air • eez) — persons sent out by a church to spread their religion in another country

nation (NAY • shun) — a group of people who share a common language, customs, beliefs, and way of life

orator (OR • ay • ter) — a person who is good at making speeches

passport (PASS • port) — a paper that is issued by a government saying that a person is a citizen of that government's country

representative (rep • rih • ZEN • ta • tiv) — a person who acts and speaks for a group of people

sachem (SAYCH • im) — a chief of an Indian nation who is a leader during times of peace

symbol (SIM • bil) — a thing that stands for something else

territory (TAIR • ih • tor • ee) — an area of land that a group of people regard as their own

totem (TOH • tim) — an animal or a natural object used by a family or other group to represent them; a symbol

traditional (truh • DISH • un • il) — following old ways or old ideas

treaty (TREE • tee) — a written agreement between two groups having to do with trade, peace, land rights, etc.

INDEX

About the Author

Jill Duvall is a political scientist who received an M.A. from Georgetown University in 1976. Since then, her research and writing have included a variety of national and international issues. Among these are world hunger, alternative energy, human rights, cross-cultural and interracial relationships. One of her current endeavors is a study of ancient goddess cultures. Ms. Duvall proudly serves as a member of the Board of Managers of the Glenn Mills Schools, a facility that is revolutionizing methods for rehabilitating male juvenile delinquents.